50 POP SONGS FOR KIDS

VIOLIN

2 Another One Bites the Dust
3 Believer
4 Call Me Maybe
6 Can't Stop the Feeling!
8 Dance Monkey
10 Don't Fear the Reaper
12 Don't Stop Believin'
7 Everything Is Awesome (Awesome Remixx!!!)
14 Feel It Still
16 Fight Song
18 Forever Young
19 Free Fallin'
20 Hallelujah
21 Happy
22 High Hopes
24 Hound Dog
26 I Don't Care
28 In the Air Tonight
30 Into the Groove
32 Into the Unknown
34 Let It Be
36 Let's Get It Started
25 Louie, Louie
38 The Middle
39 A Million Dreams

40 No Tears Left to Cry
42 Ocean Eyes
44 Old Town Road (Remix)

Rewrite the Stars
52 Scars to Your Beautiful
51 Spirit
54 Sucker
55 Surfin' U.S.A.
56 Sweet Home Alabama
58 A Thousand Miles
57 Tomorrow
60 Twist and Shout
62 Viva La Vida
64 We Are Never Ever Getting Back Together
61 We Will Rock You
66 What About Us
68 Whatever It Takes
67 Wish You Were Here
70 Y.M.C.A.
71 You Can Call Me Al
72 You Will Be Found

Available for
FLUTE, OBOE, CLARINET, ALTO SAX, TENOR SAX, TRUMPET, HORN,
TROMBONE, VIOLIN, VIOLA, CELLO, RECORDER, and MALLET PERCUSSION

ISBN 978-1-70510-741-6

HAL•LEONARD®

Contact us:
Hal Leonard
7777 West Bluemound Road
Milwaukee, WI 53213
Email: info@halleonard.com

In Europe, contact:
Hal Leonard Europe Limited
42 Wigmore Street
Marylebone, London, W1U 2RN
Email: info@halleonardeurope.com

In Australia, contact:
Hal Leonard Australia Pty. Ltd.
4 Lentara Court
Cheltenham, Victoria, 3192 Australia
Email: info@halleonard.com.au

ANOTHER ONE BITES THE DUST

VIOLIN

Words and Music by
JOHN DEACON

BELIEVER

Violin

Words and Music by DAN REYNOLDS,
WAYNE SERMON, BEN McKEE, DANIEL PLATZMAN,
JUSTIN TRANTOR, MATTIAS LARSSON and ROBIN FREDRICKSSON

CALL ME MAYBE

Violin

Words and Music by CARLY RAE JEPSEN,
JOSHUA RAMSAY and TAVISH CROWE

CAN'T STOP THE FEELING!

from TROLLS

Violin

Words and Music by JUSTIN TIMBERLAKE,
MAX MARTIN and SHELLBACK

EVERYTHING IS AWESOME
(Awesome Remixx!!!)
from THE LEGO MOVIE

VIOLIN

Words by SHAWN PATTERSON
Music by ANDREW SAMBERG,
JORMA TACCONE, AKIVA SCHAFFER,
JOSHUA BARTHOLOMEW, LISA HARRITON
and SHAWN PATTERSON

Moderately fast

DANCE MONKEY

VIOLIN

Words and Music by
TONI WATSON

Dance Pop

9

DON'T FEAR THE REAPER

VIOLIN

Words and Music by
DONALD ROESER

DON'T STOP BELIEVIN'

VIOLIN

Words and Music by STEVE PERRY,
NEAL SCHON and JONATHAN CAIN

FEEL IT STILL

Violin

Words and Music by JOHN GOURLEY,
ZACH CAROTHERS, JASON SECHRIST, ERIC HOWK,
KYLE O'QUIN, BRIAN HOLLAND, FREDDIE GORMAN,
GEORGIA DOBBINS, ROBERT BATEMAN, WILLIAM GARRETT,
JOHN HILL and ASA TACCONE

15

FIGHT SONG

VIOLIN

Words and Music by RACHEL PLATTEN
and DAVE BASSETT

FOREVER YOUNG

VIOLIN

Words and Music by ROD STEWART,
KEVIN SAVIGAR, JIM CREGAN
and BOB DYLAN

FREE FALLIN'

VIOLIN

Words and Music by TOM PETTY
and JEFF LYNNE

HALLELUJAH

VIOLIN

Words and Music by
LEONARD COHEN

HAPPY
from DESPICABLE ME 2

VIOLIN

Words and Music by
PHARRELL WILLIAMS

HIGH HOPES

VIOLIN

Words and Music by BRENDON URIE,
SAMUEL HOLLANDER, WILLIAM LOBBAN BEAN,
JONAS JEBERG, JACOB SINCLAIR,
JENNY OWEN YOUNGS, ILSEY JUBER,
LAUREN PRITCHARD and TAYLA PARX

HOUND DOG

VIOLIN

Words and Music by JERRY LEIBER
and MIKE STOLLER

LOUIE, LOUIE

VIOLIN

Words and Music by
RICHARD BERRY

I DON'T CARE

VIOLIN

Words and Music by ED SHEERAN,
JUSTIN BIEBER, FRED GIBSON,
JASON BOYD, MAX MARTIN
and SHELLBACK

Syncopated Pop

IN THE AIR TONIGHT

VIOLIN

Words and Music by
PHIL COLLINS

INTO THE GROOVE

VIOLIN

Words and Music by STEPHEN BRAY
and MADONNA CICCONE

INTO THE UNKNOWN

from FROZEN 2

VIOLIN

Music and Lyrics by KRISTEN ANDERSON-LOPEZ
and ROBERT LOPEZ

Mysteriously, in 2

LET IT BE

VIOLIN

Words and Music by JOHN LENNON
PAUL McCARTNEY

LET'S GET IT STARTED

Violin

Words and Music by WILL ADAMS,
ALLAN PINEDA, JAIME GOMEZ,
MICHAEL FRATANTUNO, GEORGE PAJON JR.
and TERENCE YOSHIAKI GRAVES

THE MIDDLE

VIOLIN

Words and Music by SARAH AARONS,
MARCUS LOMAX, JORDAN JOHNSON,
ANTON ZASLAVSKI, KYLE TREWARTHA,
MICHAEL TREWARTHA and STEFAN JOHNSON

A MILLION DREAMS

from THE GREATEST SHOWMAN

VIOLIN

Words and Music by BENJ PASEK
and JUSTIN PAUL

Moderately, with intensity

NO TEARS LEFT TO CRY

VIOLIN

Words and Music by ARIANA GRANDE,
SAVAN KOTECHA, MAX MARTIN
and ILYA

(small note optional)

OCEAN EYES

VIOLIN

Words and Music by
FINNEAS O'CONNELL

PERFECT

VIOLIN

Words and Music by
ED SHEERAN

OLD TOWN ROAD
(Remix)

VIOLIN

Words and Music by TRENT REZNOR,
BILLY RAY CYRUS, JOCELYN DONALD,
ATTICUS ROSS, KIOWA ROUKEMA
and MONTERO LAMAR HILL

PARTY IN THE U.S.A.

VIOLIN

Words and Music by JESSICA CORNISH,
LUKASZ GOTTWALD and CLAUDE KELLY

Moderate Pop

PROUD MARY

VIOLIN

Words and Music by
JOHN FOGERTY

RESPECT

VIOLIN

Words and Music by
OTIS REDDING

Moderately

REWRITE THE STARS
from THE GREATEST SHOWMAN

VIOLIN

Words and Music by BENJ PASEK
and JUSTIN PAUL

SPIRIT
from THE LION KING 2019

Violin

Written by TIMOTHY McKENZIE,
ILYA SALMANZADEH and BEYONCÉ

SCARS TO YOUR BEAUTIFUL

Violin

Words and Music by ALESSIA CARACCIOLO,
WARREN FELDER, COLERIDGE TILLMAN
and ANDREW WANSEL

SUCKER

VIOLIN

Words and Music by NICK JONAS,
JOSEPH JONAS, MILES ALE,
MUSTAFA AHMED, RYAN TEDDER,
LOUIS BELL, ADAM FEENEY,
KEVIN JONAS and HOMER STEINWEISS

SURFIN' U.S.A.

VIOLIN

Words and Music by
CHUCK BERRY

Solid Shuffle beat

SWEET HOME ALABAMA

Violin

Words and Music by RONNIE VAN ZANT,
ED KING and GARY ROSSINGTON

TOMORROW
from the Musical Production ANNIE

VIOLIN

Lyric by MARTIN CHARNIN
Music by CHARLES STROUSE

A THOUSAND MILES

VIOLIN

Words and Music by
VANESSA CARLTON

TWIST AND SHOUT

VIOLIN

Words and Music by BERT RUSSELL
and PHIL MEDLEY

WE WILL ROCK YOU

VIOLIN

Words and Music by
BRIAN MAY

VIVA LA VIDA

VIOLIN

Words and Music by GUY BERRYMAN,
JON BUCKLAND, WILL CHAMPION
and CHRIS MARTIN

Moderately

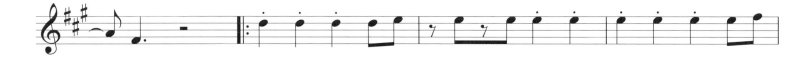

WE ARE NEVER EVER GETTING BACK TOGETHER

Violin

Words and Music by TAYLOR SWIFT,
MAX MARTIN and SHELLBACK

65

WHAT ABOUT US

VIOLIN

Words and Music by ALECIA MOORE,
STEVE MAC and JOHNNY McDAID

WISH YOU WERE HERE

VIOLIN

Words and Music by ROGER WATERS
and DAVID GILMOUR

WHATEVER IT TAKES

Violin

Words and Music by DAN REYNOLDS,
WAYNE SERMON, BEN McKEE,
DANIEL PLATZMAN and JOEL LITTLE

Y.M.C.A.

VIOLIN

Words and Music by JACQUES MORALI,
HENRI BELOLO and VICTOR WILLIS

YOU CAN CALL ME AL

VIOLIN

Words and Music by
PAUL SIMON

Moderately fast

YOU WILL BE FOUND

from DEAR EVAN HANSEN

VIOLIN

Music and Lyrics by BENJ PASEK
and JUSTIN PAUL